# BIRTHING KINGS

Kyna Kemp

© 2017 Kyna Kemp
All rights reserved.

ISBN: **0-9993431-0-6**
ISBN 13: **978-0-9993431-0-4**
Library of Congress Control Number: **XXXXX (If applicable)**
LCCN Imprint Name: **City and State (If applicable)**

# **DEDICATION**

To all the mothers who have had the privilege of giving birth to preemie babies, your love, strength, and tenacity will provide your babies with everything they need to survive.

# ACKNOWLEDGEMENTS

Special thank you to my husband, Raymond Kemp, who walked with me through this journey. Thank you for comforting me, holding me up, and providing a shoulder to cry on. Thank you for pushing me to go after my dreams and supporting me in the process. I love you more than you know.

To my parents, Coleman and Sonia Starks, thank you for your unconditional love, prayers, and support. If it were not for you, I would not be alive to share my story with the world. Thank you for everything that you do for my family and me. Words cannot express my love and appreciation for you.

To my family and friends, thank you for your calls, texts, gifts of love, and prayers. My family and I truly appreciate your thoughtfulness.

# **CONTENTS**

Introduction ................................................................... 6

My First Pregnancy ........................................................ 8

Oh No! It's Too Early ................................................... 11

It's Time ....................................................................... 14

Can I Still Breastfeed? ................................................. 17

Justin's Home .............................................................. 19

Second Time Around .................................................. 26

Oh No! Not Again ....................................................... 29

C-Section ..................................................................... 31

Life in the NICU .......................................................... 35

Asa's Home ................................................................. 41

Life Today ................................................................... 45

Resources for Parents of Premature Babies ................ 48

Notes ........................................................................... 49

# Introduction

Being able to birth a child is definitely a gift from God. Growing up, I often dreamed about getting married, purchasing a home, and having a family. I wanted two children, a son and a daughter, five years apart. Like most women, I looked forward to motherhood and celebrating the momentous occasion with family and friends. In my dreams, everything was perfect. My pregnancies were flawless, and I birthed two healthy children naturally. In reality, both pregnancies started off wonderful with minimal morning sickness and cravings. However, during the eighth month of my first pregnancy and the seventh month of my second, the unexpected happened. My water broke, and I ended up giving birth to not one but two children born prematurely. Even though these events occurred seven years apart, both were stressful and emotional times for my family.

So what is premature birth? Premature birth is a birth that occurs before the thirty-seventh week of pregnancy. According to the March of Dimes, 15 million babies are born prematurely each year around the world, and 1 million will die.[1] Preterm birth is the number-one cause of death among babies and leading cause of lifelong disabilities. Depending on the complications surrounding the premature birth, this will determine what types of treatment will be administered to the baby as well as how long the baby will have to stay in the Nursery Intensive Care Unit, often referred to as the NICU. Even after the baby is discharged from the hospital, a series of

---

[1] March of Dimes is a United States nonprofit organization that works to improve the health of mothers and babies by preventing birth defects, premature birth and infant mortality. For more information, visit the website www.marchofdimes.org.

programs and appointments are available for preterm babies to ensure their growth and development stay on track.

Although this was not the journey I had planned, God saw fit to take me through this experience in order to share it with you. As you read this book, you will experience a detailed account of what I went through to bring my wonderful sons into this world. Despite the differences in each occurrence, my sons survived and are excelling in life today. With the combination of the love, strength, and tenacity, your family and you can survive too.

# **My First Pregnancy**

At the age of thirty-two, after becoming extremely sick at work, I learned I was pregnant with my first child on July 5, 2006. At that time, I was working two jobs and finishing up my master's degree program at the University of Phoenix, Sacramento Campus. I purchased a salad for lunch, and shortly after eating it, I began to feel nauseated. I ran to the bathroom, and needless to say, I remained there for almost thirty minutes.

I went home early from work and purchased a pregnancy test. After receiving the test results, I called my husband and told him that his father was right. I was pregnant. Ironically, the day before we had family and friends over for a bar-b-que, and my father-in-law saw me and asked my husband if I was pregnant, and he said "No".

I called my obstetrician and set up an appointment to be seen. My husband and I went to the appointment, filled out all of the paperwork, and answered all the nurse's questions. Based on the date of my last menstrual cycle, I was given a due date of February 23, 2007. Once that was complete, I was put on a monthly appointment rotation. We notified the family that there would soon be a new grandchild on both sides of the family.

Everyone was excited. So was I, but I was also nervous. I knew lots of women who had children, but this was my first experience. I notified my boss but told her that she had to keep it a secret until I reached the end of my first trimester. She agreed.

My pregnancy was going well, as I only experienced morning sickness twice. I was eating right, attending my monthly appointments, and still working a full and a part-time job. My husband and I attended some birthing and breastfeeding classes. At the five-month mark, we found out that we were having a son. I was very happy because I had always wanted my first child to be a boy.

I thought this pregnancy was easy. My only craving was spicy chicken wings from my neighborhood Chinese restaurant. It was bad. Every time I called to order, they knew me by name. I really was not showing, as I carried in the lower part of my abdomen. Most of my coworkers did not know I was pregnant.

Just when I thought I could make it two more months, everything changed. On Saturday, December 30, 2006, I worked from eight to noon at my part-time job and then went to meet my family at Joe's Crab Shack for lunch. After lunch, I went home to rest before going to the Sacramento Kings game with my sisters and grandmother, who was visiting from South Carolina. At the game, my sister and I shared some garlic fries. Afterward, I dropped off everyone and then went home.

The next morning, Sunday, December 31, 2006, I woke up with the worse cramps. They finally calmed down, so I got ready for church. My church was having a Christmas revival, and I wanted to attend.

All through the church service, I felt uncomfortable. I went to the altar for prayer, and the guest speaker and his wife prayed for me. I felt a little better after the prayer. I went home and took a nap. That evening we were going to attend Watch Night service.

As we were getting ready for church, my sister-in-law called to see what we were doing. She and my father-in-law were making gumbo and said we should stop by after church. My father-in-law asked how I was doing. I said I was fine. Anyone who knows me knows I will always say I'm fine even if I'm not. I'm not sure how my father-in-law knew, but after my conversation with him, he told my sister-in-law that I was going to have the baby.

She said, "No, the baby is not due yet."

He simply said, "Okay."

My husband and I went to Watch Night service, and I sang in the choir as usual. After service, I was exhausted, so we went home.

# Oh No! It's Too Early

At five thirty in the morning on January 1, 2007, I was awakened, as I felt like I was urinating on myself. I sat up for a minute and then ran to the bathroom. I sat there until the sensation finally stopped.

I thought, "Oh no! Something is wrong. I'm not due until February."

I grabbed the phone and called the advice nurse. She asked a series of questions and then said, "I think you should come in and be seen."

I woke up my husband and informed him that I believed my water had just broken. He tried to go back to sleep, but I told him that we really needed to go to the hospital. We got dressed and went to the hospital.

When we got there, I was examined right away and informed that my water had indeed broken and I had to stay in the hospital until I had the baby. It could be a day, a week, or even multiple weeks until the baby came, but I had to remain in the hospital. Also in the event that the baby did come before the thirty-fifth week, this hospital did not have the equipment to care for a premature baby, so an ambulance was going to transport me to another hospital that did.

I started to panic. It was January 1, 2007, and I was not due until February 23, 2007. All sorts of thoughts began to flood my mind.

I pondered, "My baby could not possibly come this early. Would he survive if he were born this early? Would his brain and lungs be fully developed and functioning properly?"

My other concerns were that we did not have any of the baby supplies, nor was the baby's room set up. Originally, my husband and I had planned to go shopping for the crib, stroller, and car seats on January 1, 2007. But the baby had other plans for us. My husband ensured me that everything was going to be all right, and he started to call the family to let them know what was going on.

The nurse came in to inform me that the paramedics were in route to transport me to the other hospital. I asked the nurse if I could ride with my husband to the hospital instead of in an ambulance, but she told me "No", because if I went into labor while in route to the hospital, the paramedics were equipped to handle an emergency situation. So I was prepared for transport and taken to another facility. My new room was so small that I could barely move around in it. The check-in desk was right outside the door, and I could hear everything going on in the hallway.

My family and close friends began to arrive. They rotated in and out the whole day. Visiting hours were over at nine o'clock. After everyone left, it was just my husband and me. As we were sitting in the room watching television, my mind started to wander. My husband asked if I was all right. I started crying. Fear had set in, and I was in full panic mode. He consoled me and told me not to worry about anything. Our family had gone out and purchased baby items for us. So, I did not need to worry about anything. My husband reassured me that it was going to be okay.

I was in such a panic that I could not even pray. My husband called my parents, who prayed for me over the phone. I felt a sense of relief after that.

I tried to sleep, but as soon as I started to relax, I began to have contractions. I was hooked up to all sorts of monitors and just could not seem to get comfortable. The only comfortable position was on my side.

As the cramps got worse, I began to vomit. The nurse came in, adjusted the monitor, and pretty much told me I had to stop moving around. I was in pain, and she had the nerve to tell me to stop moving. I finally could not take it anymore, and I instructed my husband to find me another nurse.

A little while later, another nurse came in the room, who informed me that she would be taking care of me for the rest of the evening. The contractions began to come faster, but when the doctor checked, I was only six centimeters dilated.

I began to shout, "Oh, God, I need you!"

The next person to come in the room was the anesthesiologist, who asked if I wanted an epidural. After I said yes, he explained the procedure and proceeded to give me the epidural. I then fell asleep. The next thing I knew, I was being wheeled into the delivery room, and my parents were standing there with my husband.

# It's Time

The doctor said, "It's time to have the baby." But before I started to push, the doctor told us, "Your baby probably won't come out screaming because his lungs are not fully developed at thirty-two weeks gestation."

My husband and I said ok. At 4:44 a.m. on January 2, 2007, after just a few pushes, a baby boy came out screaming. We all said his lungs were working just fine. He weighed in at three pounds and thirteen ounces, and he was 15.1 inches long. My husband named him Justin Mekhi Kemp. They rushed off Justin to clean him up and take him to the NICU, a nursery where specialized doctors and nurses provide twenty-four-hour care for sick or premature babies.

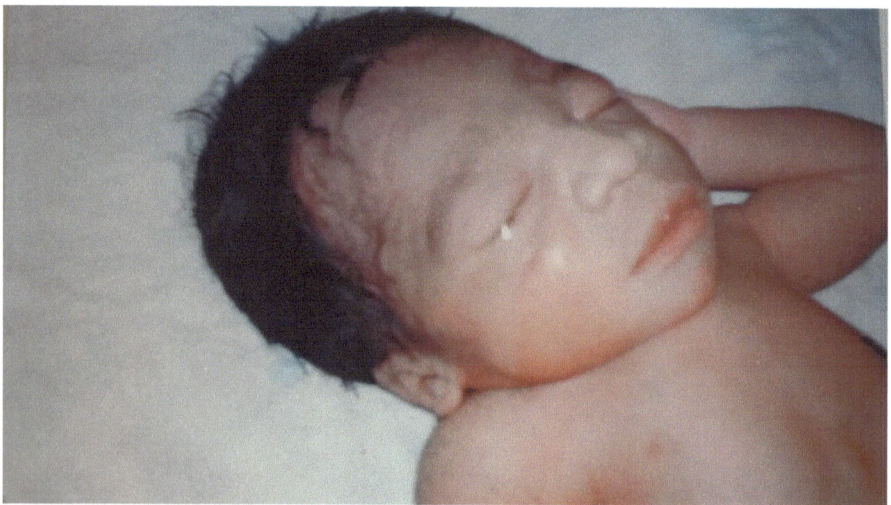

My husband went with the nurse, while the doctor cleaned me up and took me to recovery. Since I did not have a history of premature birth in my family, a pathologist would examine my placenta to determine why Justin came so early. But he was unable to make a finding, as my placenta showed no irregularities.

After about two hours in the recovery room, I was moved to another room for the remainder of my stay. Since Justin was born prematurely, he had to the stay in the NICU and could not be brought to my room. I wanted to see my baby, so my husband requested a wheelchair and wheeled me down to the NICU to see him.

When we entered the room, the nurses told us to wash our hands before we could touch the baby. When we first entered the NICU, it seemed dark and cold to me. Justin was lying in an incubator with all types of monitors hooked up to him. I didn't know what to think. I began to feel like I had done something wrong to cause Justin to come early.

The nurses explained what was going on, including the call-in and visiting procedures. The doctors and nurses ensured me that NICU was the safest place for Justin to be and encouraged me to ask questions and express my concerns, which helped ease my mind.

Eighteen hours after delivery, I was being discharged from the hospital, but I could not take my baby home with me. One of the hardest things I had to do was leave the hospital without my baby.

Over the first couple days, Justin lost weight and became jaundiced, a condition common in preterm babies that causes the yellowing of the skin. The nurses explained that high bilirubin levels cause jaundice and that light therapy treats the condition. It took about two days for the jaundice to go away once the light therapy started.

While Justin was being treated for jaundice, I was not able to hold or feed him. The nurses learned very quickly that Justin did not like pacifiers. Every time they would give him a pacifier, he would spit it out. Justin would self-soothe by sucking on his own tongue.

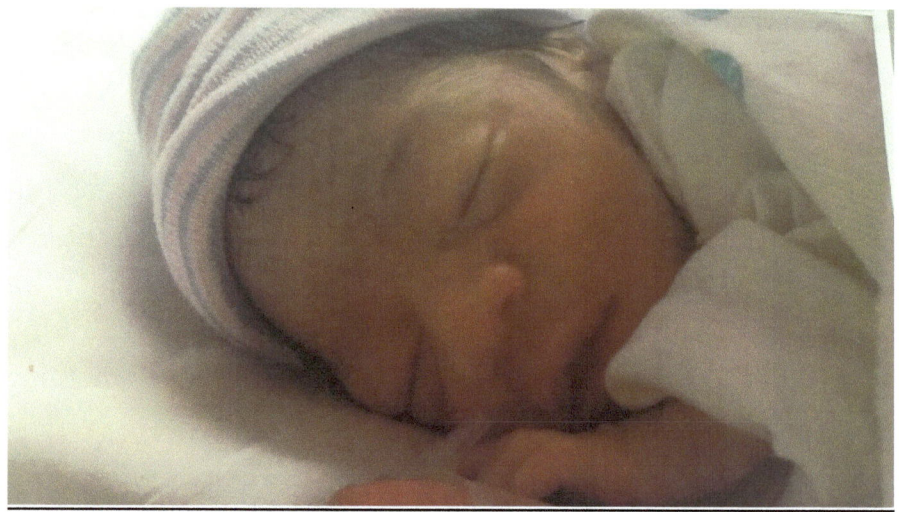

# Can I Still Breastfeed?

I asked a lot of questions about the feedings and the possibility of breastfeeding. Before Justin was born, I had planned to breastfeed, but with him being in the hospital, that was going to be hard. I talked to one of the nurses, and she told me that breast milk would be the most beneficial in helping Justin grow and suggested I get a breast pump. My husband bought me a portable pump, and I began to use it every three hours to help stimulate the milk.

When I first started pumping, my breasts became so engorged that they hurt, but I did not produce a lot of milk. I began to stress because I was concerned that my baby would not get the nutrients that he needed to grow. During this time, I was very emotional and cried a lot.

At my next visit with Justin, I expressed my concerns with the nurse, and she asked one of the lactation consultants to come and talk with me. She was very nice and understanding. She told me to make sure I took the following steps: eat well-balanced meals; drink lots of water; make sure I was in a relaxing environment before pumping; focus on good thoughts; and remain calm.

Right before she left the room, she told me, "Do not give up because your baby is depending on you."

I took her advice, and it really worked. Within a week, I started to produce more milk. Every day when I went to the NICU, I would take the milk with me, and the nurses would use it to feed Justin. The nurses gave me little bottles to place the milk in. Each bottle had to be labeled with Justin's name and the date, as the breast milk was stored in the NICU freezer.

As the nurses increased Justin's milk intake, he began to have reflux for a few days, so the nurses decreased his intake. Once Justin was able to digest the milk well, the ounces increased, and he began to gain weight. In order for Justin to be discharged from the hospital, he had to be able to do the following: breathe on his own; drink and digest milk at each feeding without reflux; and weigh at least five pounds. After two weeks, Justin finally met all the requirements to be discharged and was able to come home.

# Justin's Home

One of the happiest days of my life was when Justin was released from the hospital. We were so excited to finally have him home that we did not have any family over the first week. We wanted to bond with Justin and get used to his new environment. When we started to have family and friends over, before they could hold Justin, they could not be sick and they had to wash their hands. We had soap and hand sanitizer in every room of the house.

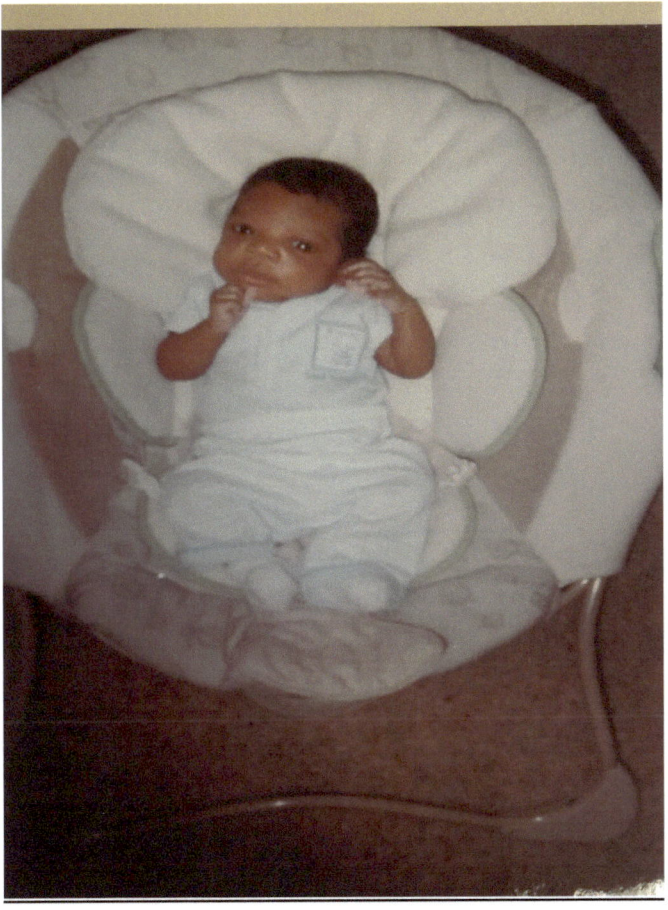

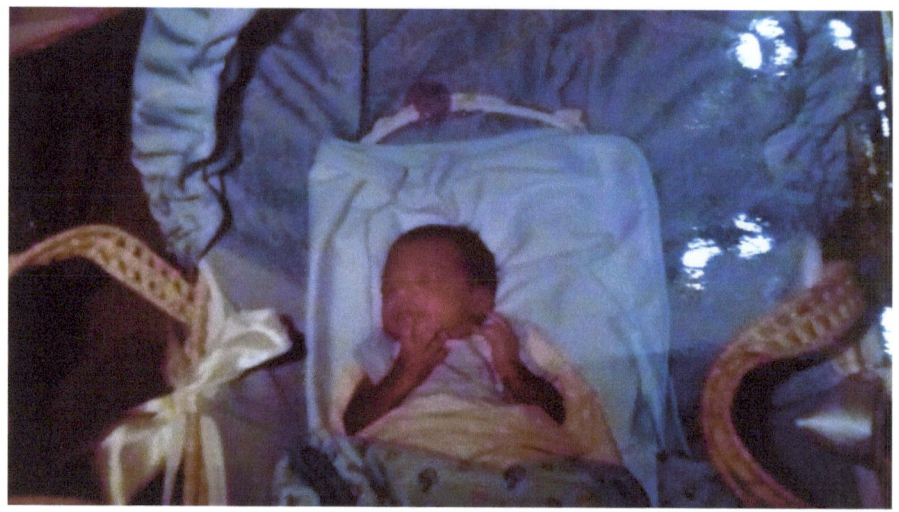

The first few weeks after Justin came home were very emotional for me. I did not really know what was going on, but many days I felt overwhelmed and would just cry for no reason. I began to doubt myself as a mother and did not feel equipped to take care of my baby. This was my first child, and he was so small and fragile. It took some time to become acclimated to Justin waking up every three hours and trying to sleep while he was. There were a lot of sleepless days and nights. My husband made sure I rested and got out of the house so I would not go crazy.

Just as we were trying to get a routine set up, my father-in-law passed away unexpectedly and never got to meet Justin. This was a stressful time for our family. I was very emotional and did not think I could handle anymore unexpected events. Looking back on it now, I'm not sure if I suffered from baby blues or postpartum depression, a depression that women can suffer from after having a baby. But I did go through depression. I did not tell my doctor or get professional help, but being surrounded by my loving family really helped me to hold it together in order to be there for my baby.

At Justin's first doctor appointment, we learned that premature babies often have two ages: chronological (the age from the day of birth) and adjusted (the age of the baby based on his due date). At each appointment, the doctor charted Justin's weight, length, and head circumference and would compare the numbers on the chronological and adjusted charts to determine if he were growing correctly.

As part of the hospital's protocol for premature babies, Justin was referred to the Alta Regional Program, which provides early intervention to enhance the growth and development in children. Justin had a series of appointments with his primary care physician, occupational and physical therapists, and specialty doctors in the High-Risk Infant Follow-Up Clinic.

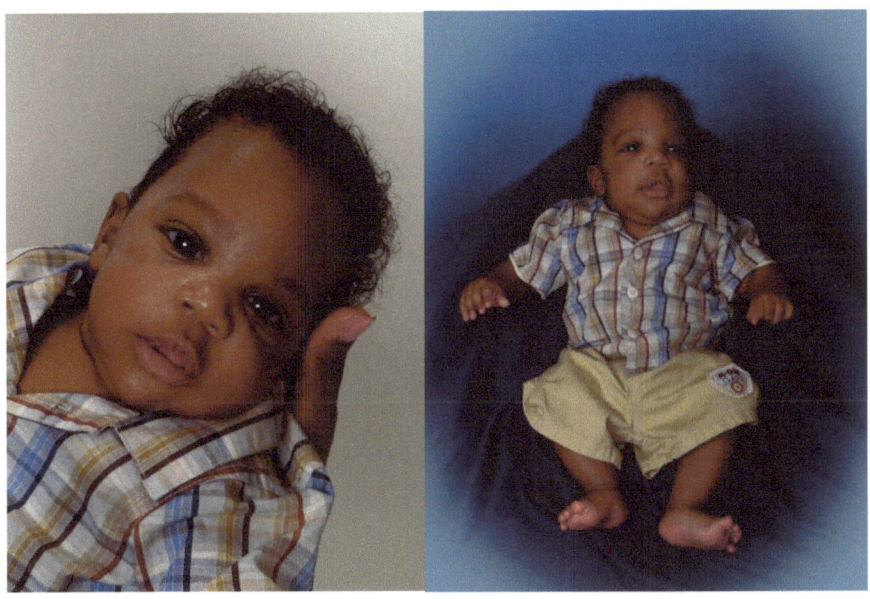

Every six months, the doctors tested Justin's growth and development. I went back to work when Justin was five months old. I was very nervous about leaving my son. A friend of the family had an in-home daycare, and she started watching Justin for us on a full-time basis. On his first day, I provided the daycare provider with food, extra clothes, and three pages of dos and don'ts for Justin.

The daycare provider just laughed when she read it. She said, "I have been taking care of kids for a long time. I know what to do."

I knew she would take good care of Justin, but I just wanted to make sure.

The Kemp Family
2007

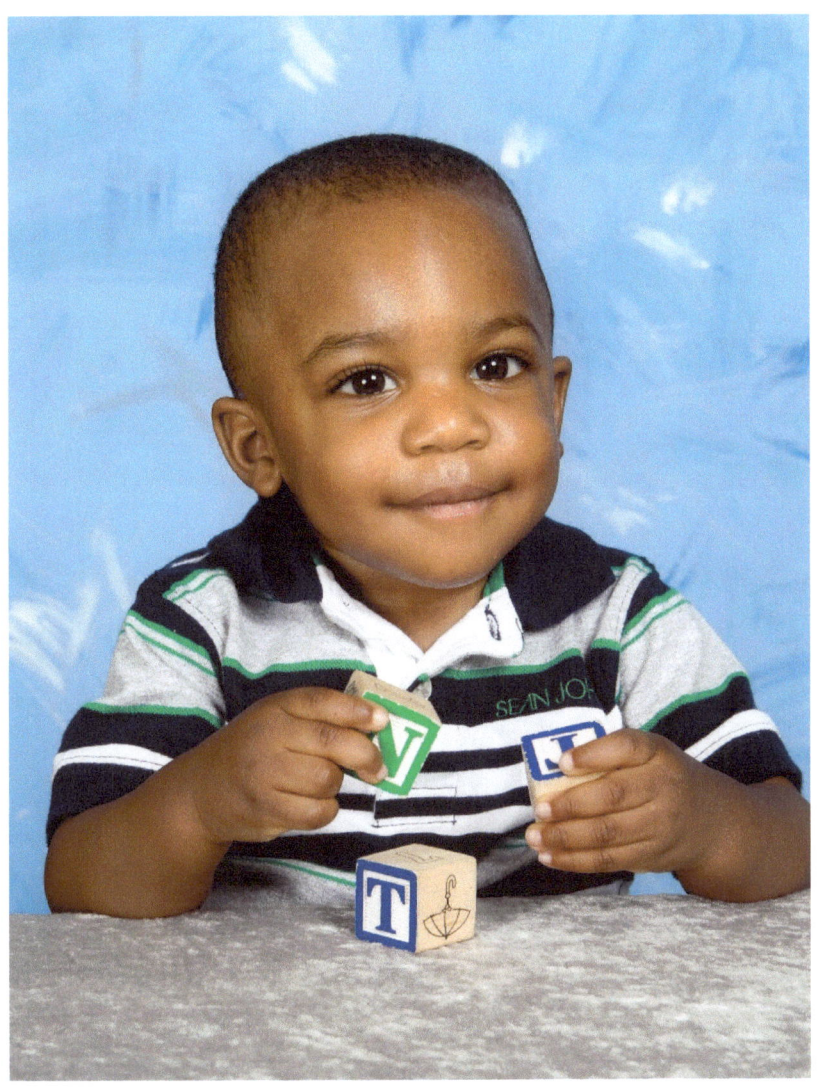

When Justin was one-year old, he began to learn how to walk. He started out walking on his toes, often referred to as toe walking. After several appointments with the physical therapists, they determined that Justin had cerebral palsy and would need braces on his legs to help him walk.

I was in complete shock. "Cerebral palsy," I thought. "Really?"

I prayed and told the Lord I was not accepting that diagnosis. Walking on your toes was nothing new to my family. My father, brother, uncle, and cousins all walk on their toes. The physical therapist told us to get high-top tennis shoes to help strengthen Justin's ankles as well as referred us to a specialist who would fit Justin for the braces.

We went to the appointment, and the specialist watched Justin walk. After careful examination, he determined that Justin did not need braces and recommended keeping Justin in high-top shoes as much as possible. Justin went from walking to running in a matter of weeks. After the two-year mark, Justin was considered to be on right on track according to all the charts and graphs.

The daycare provider was instrumental in Justin's early learning of his alphabet and numbers. At night, we would practice his alphabet and read his favorite books. By the age of three, Justin was potty-trained and went from the in-home daycare to preschool. Once there, Justin really started to blossom.

On June 14, 2012, Justin graduated from preschool and started kindergarten in August 2012, where he made the honor roll all three trimesters.

In 2013, when Justin was six years old, my husband and I made the decision we wanted to have another child.

# Second Time Around

At the beginning of November 2013, I noticed that certain scents made me feel nauseated. On November 20, 2013, I found out I was pregnant with my second child. Once my doctor confirmed the news, my husband and I notified the family that there would soon be another grandchild. I was excited, as I did not want Justin to be an only child. However, at the same time, I was also nervous about the possibility of having another premature child.

I consulted with my doctor, and she told me that, starting at twenty weeks' gestation, I would be given progesterone injections each week to help prevent the baby from coming prematurely. Although I was not excited about getting shots weekly, I was happy that was a remedy to keep me pregnant longer.

Overall my pregnancy was similar to the first one, seldom having morning sickness or cravings. However, this time around, I was dealing with a breathing issue. In 2013, I was diagnosed with a condition called "Subglottic Stenosis," the narrowing of the airway below the vocal cords right above the trachea. The only treatment is a surgical procedure called direct laryngoscopy dilation, which consists of me being put to sleep and the doctor placing a scope with a balloon on the end through my nose and into my throat. Once in my throat, he would inflate the balloon several times to open my windpipe. At some point during my pregnancy, I was going to need another surgical procedure. After several discussions, my throat specialist and ob-gyn decided that the best time for the procedure would be before the end of my twentieth week of pregnancy.

On February 4, 2014, I went in for my second throat dilation, which was a traumatic experience. This time, in an effort to have an open airway during the rest of my pregnancy, the doctor used the scope with the balloon to widen my airway as well as a laser to get rid of excess cartilage. Since this was an outpatient surgery, I was discharged from the hospital later that afternoon.

Soon after I got home, I started coughing and could not catch my breath. As a result, air pockets formed in my throat, causing it to swell. My husband took me back to the hospital, where I was admitted to the ICU and remained there for three days. I was taken off work for two weeks and placed on a round of antibiotics and steroids. This was an extremely scary experience for my unborn child and me.

Despite going through this, my pregnancy was progressing. On February 25, 2014, we found out that I was having another son. At this point, I also started receiving the painful progesterone injections every week in my hips in an effort to reduce premature birth.

Everything was going well until March 30, 2014, when my fluid began to leak out. Concerned, I called my doctor and was told to come in right away. She examined me and said there was still enough fluid around the baby, but if I began to leak more, I was to come back in. Every day, a little more fluid would gush out. It was to the point that I had to wear maxi pads every day.

Worried, I went back to the doctor on April 2, 2014. The doctor examined me again and said there was still enough fluid around the baby. I continued to work and go to church, but it was very uncomfortable, as the fluid had begun to gush out more frequently.

# Oh No! Not Again

On Thursday, April 10, 2014, l left work early for my scheduled checkup, and as soon as I got out of the car, my water broke. I checked in at the desk and let the receptionist know that my water had just broken on my way into the office. She notified my doctor, and I was examined right away. Sure enough, this time my water was completely broken. So, I was going to be admitted to the hospital. My doctor called Labor and Delivery to let them know that I was on my way. I called my husband and told him to meet me at the hospital because I was being admitted. He notified the family.

I arrived at Labor and Delivery and was checked in immediately. The concern was that I was only twenty-eight weeks pregnant, which meant I would be in the hospital until the baby came. This hospital did not have a NICU, so I would have to be transported to another facility again.

However, this time the hospital where I was supposed to be transported to did not have any available beds. The nurses called around to some of the other hospitals in the network, but the only one with availability was in Walnut Creek, which is about one hour and thirty minutes from Sacramento. I told them that I was not going to Walnut Creek. All my family was in Sacramento. Justin had to get to school every day, and that was too far to drive. So, after my refusal to be transported out of town, it was decided that I would be moved to a hospital outside of the network until there was availability at the local hospital.

As the nurses prepared me for transport, my husband and dad updated the family on what was going on. I was taken to the other hospital and checked into my room. Around nine o'clock, shortly after I arrived, my family began to come in. They stayed for a little while and then went home. The doctors came in, examined me, and asked a lot of questions. I was hooked up to all sorts of monitors, and it was pretty hard to rest with the nurses coming in every three hours to check my vitals.

On Friday, April 11, 2014, the doctor came in and checked me a few times, but there was no change. My husband and family spent the day with me in the hospital. On Saturday, April 12, 2014, the doctor came in and examined me. He said a spot had opened up at the local hospital in my network and I was going to be transported that afternoon.

I was then moved to the local hospital and checked in. My family met me there. I was hooked back up to all the monitors, and things seemed okay, or so I thought. During the night, the nurses kept adjusting the monitors, but they would not tell me what was going on.

# C-Section

Early Sunday morning, April 13, 2014, the doctor came in and said they were concerned about the baby because the heart rate did not seem as strong throughout the night. The doctor wanted to consult with another physician first before a final decision was made. My uncle had just arrived with breakfast, but the nurse advised me not to eat anything yet. There was a possibility that I was going to be prepped for delivery sooner than later.

About thirty minutes later, a team of doctors came and told me that they wanted to do a C-section because no fluid was surrounding the baby and they could not hear the heartbeat. I asked the doctor, "why I couldn't have the baby naturally, like I did with Justin". The doctor responded, "there is a possibility the baby could go into distress while I was pushing, then they would have to do an emergency C-section, which could cause more stress on the baby."

I was not happy, but reluctantly I agreed to have the C-section. However, I told the doctor that they had to wait until my husband arrived at the hospital. As soon as the doctor left, I called my husband to let him know what was going on. He got Justin up, and they arrived at the hospital. Then I contacted my family to inform them as well. I began to cry and pray, asking God for a safe delivery and for my baby to be all right.

My family arrived as the nurses began to prep me. At eleven in the morning, I was taken into the delivery room. The team of doctors were moving about in the delivery room preparing for the C-section. One of the doctors from the team asked me, "what type of music do you like?" I told him, "gospel music." Then he asked, "what channel would you like to listen to on Pandora?" I responded, "the Tamela Mann channel". Once the music started to play, I closed my eyes, prayed and began to meditate on the songs as I was given an epidural. The doctors and nurses in the room hummed along as the music played.

As the doctor began to do the C-section, she told us that most of the baby's organs might not be fully functional since it was still early. We just said, "Okay." The doctor proceeded to cut me open and pulled out the baby. He came out screaming, just like Justin. My husband named him Asa Elias Kemp.

The nurses cleaned up Asa, then weighed him, and took him straight to the NICU. Asa weighed two pounds and thirteen ounces. And he was 15.3 inches long. My husband went with the nurse and the baby while I was cleaned up and taken to the recovery room. My placenta would be examined again in an effort to determine a cause for the premature labor. The results showed no irregularities.

After about two hours in recovery, the nurse awakened me and transferred me to a different room, where my family was waiting for me. My husband took family members one at a time down to the NICU to see Asa. The rule was that only two people could visit in the room at a time. That evening after the family left, my husband took me to the NICU to see our baby.

Asa looked so small lying in the incubator. The first thing I noticed was that Asa was hooked up to the following equipment that was different from our experience with Justin:

1. CPAP, or continuous positive airway pressure, which sends air and oxygen to a baby's lungs through small tubes in his or her nose or windpipe.
2. G-tube, or gastric feeding tube, which sends liquids into a baby's stomach for feeding when a baby is not able to take food by mouth

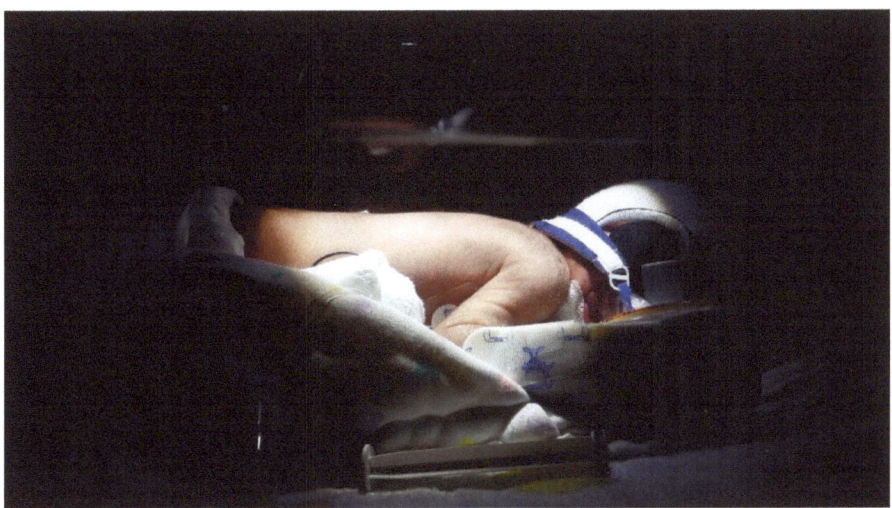

The nurse working with Asa came over, introduced herself, and explained the call-in and visitation process. She also told us about the equipment that Asa was hooked up to. I was discharged from the hospital three days after giving birth, but I was given a mothering room for an additional two days. Yet again, I had to leave without my baby.

This time it was a little harder since I had a C-section. I now had an incision that I had to keep clean and dry. I also could not lift more than ten pounds and could not drive for at least a week. My husband and family jumped in to make sure I was resting and that Justin, who was now seven years old, got to and from school, had help with homework, and was taken to martial arts practice twice a week. Since Asa was in the NICU,

Justin was not allowed to see his brother right away, which was very disappointing for him. Justin really wanted to meet his new little brother.

# Life in the NICU

The hospital was about thirty minutes from where I lived. The first week, my husband drove me to the hospital every day. We would stay until about noon, and then we would leave before the traffic got too bad. Once I was able to drive, I made sure I was there every morning for his 9:00 a.m. feeding. Asa had several nurses who cared for him, but Rita was one of the best nurses he had. She was very informative and kept me abreast of any concerns or changes.

The nurses had Asa on a feeding schedule of every three hours. During this time, I was able to change his diapers, feed him, and hold him during the first hour of my visit. Rita advised me that skin-to-skin contact was good for the babies to help adjust being out of the womb, so after Asa's feedings, I would place him inside my shirt and lay him on my chest. I was able to hold and comfort him while the sound of my heartbeat would put him right to sleep. After about an hour, Asa had to go back in the incubator.

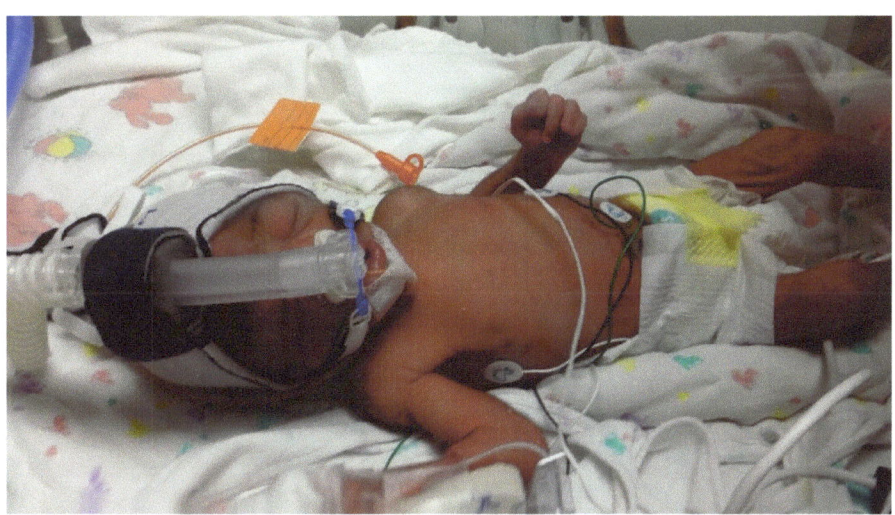

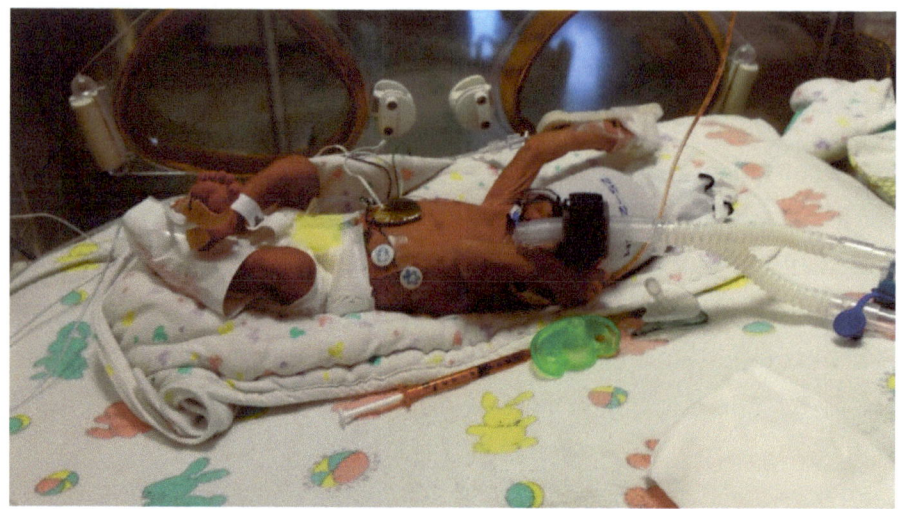

Asa did not like the CPAP machine. Every time the nurse would adjust it, he would push it off his face. After about five days, the doctor determined that Asa was breathing on his own and removed the CPAP machine, as it was no longer needed. Similar to Justin, Asa would spit out the pacifier and self-soothe himself by sucking on his own tongue.

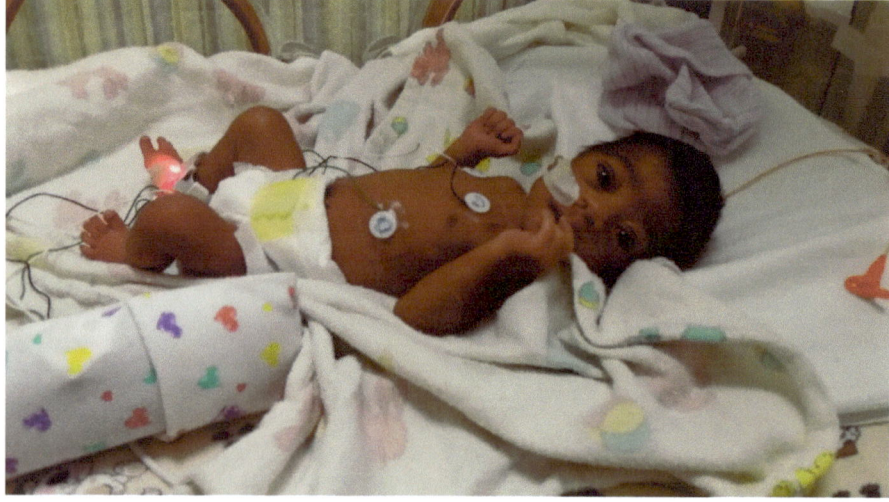

Each day Asa was dressed in outfits and hats that were made and donated to the hospital for premature babies. Every day as I visited Asa, I would see several doctors doing their rounds to check on the babies in the NICU. The doctors would say hello as they entered the room, but they would not come over and examine or update me on Asa's condition.

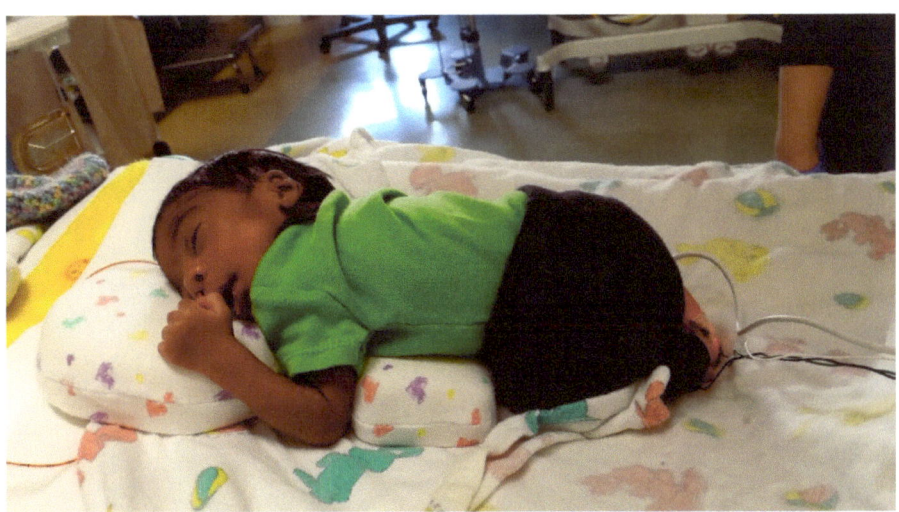

One morning, I finally asked the nurse if she could let the doctor know that I wanted to speak with him. He came over and greeted me. I asked him, "why don't you ever examine Asa and provide updates during while I am here." The doctor said, "Asa was not considered a sick baby. He was just small. When you see us doing rounds, we come to see the sickest babies first. Then we examine all the other babies." Once he told me this, I felt a little better.

On April 27, 2014, after several conversations with the nurses, Justin was finally able to meet his little brother. Justin was surprised at how small Asa was, but he was excited to see him.

I had planned to breastfeed, but since Asa was in the hospital, I knew I had to pump my breast. I still had my breast pump that I used with Justin, and I was also given one from the hospital. It took a few days for my milk to come in, but once it did, I had a good supply that I would take to the hospital. The nurses were giving Asa a special formula for premature babies and would supplement it with the breast milk. The nurses gave me little bottles and labels for my breast milk and would store it in the refrigerator to feed Asa throughout the day. Also after my skin-to-skin time with Asa, I was also able to pump in the NICU in an effort to provide more milk for Asa.

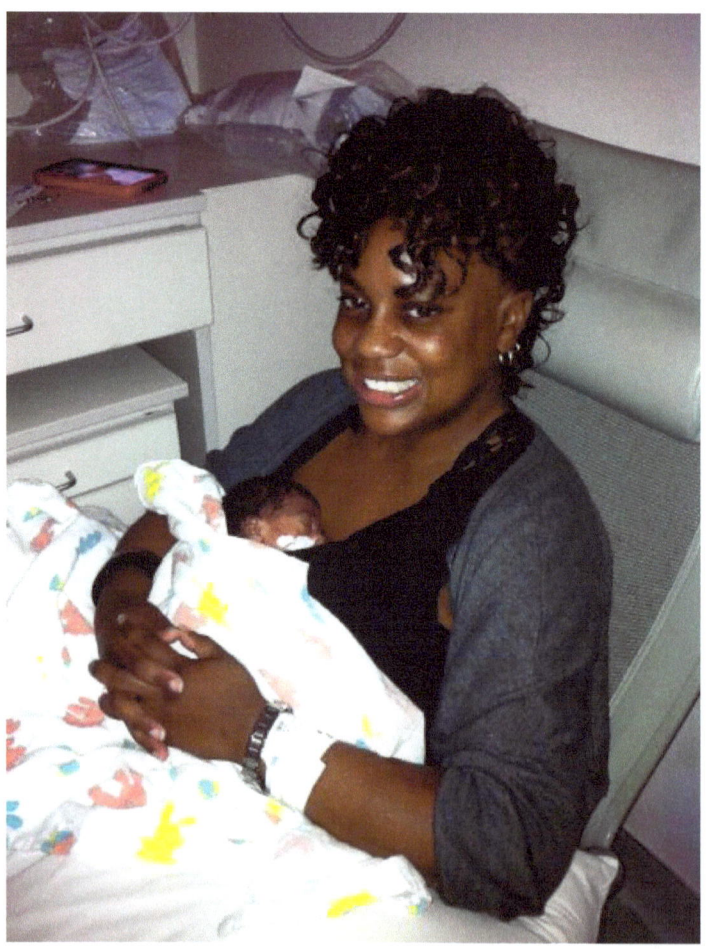

As the nurses began to increase Asa's breast milk intake, he had reflux. It took him a few weeks to be able to digest a larger amount of breast milk. Asa stayed at this hospital for three weeks. On May 6, 2014, he was transported to a hospital closer to home. Now that Asa was going to be closer to home, I could make several trips to the hospital throughout the day, and more members of the family would be able to visit.

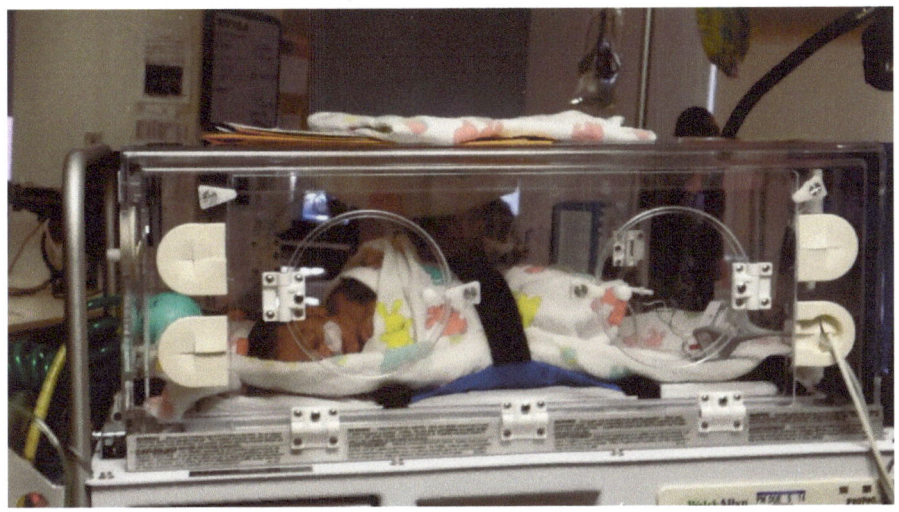

Asa was starting to gain weight and eat more, which was a good sign. Then one morning after I arrived at the hospital, the doctor did his rounds and said there were some concerns about Asa's white blood cell count being too low. The doctor wanted to do a blood transfusion. I was in total shock, so I called my husband and told him that he had to come to the hospital immediately because they wanted Asa to have a blood transfusion.

Once my husband arrived at the hospital, the nurses and doctor explained the whole process, which would take four to five hours. After all my questions were answered, I signed the authorization forms. I notified the family to let them know what was going on.

After we prayed for Asa, my husband and I left as they started the procedure. We went to lunch and then went home. I tried to rest, but my mind would not let me. After we picked up Justin from school, we went back to the hospital. As we entered the room, my dad was sitting with Asa. The procedure was still in process, but the doctors said that Asa was responding well.

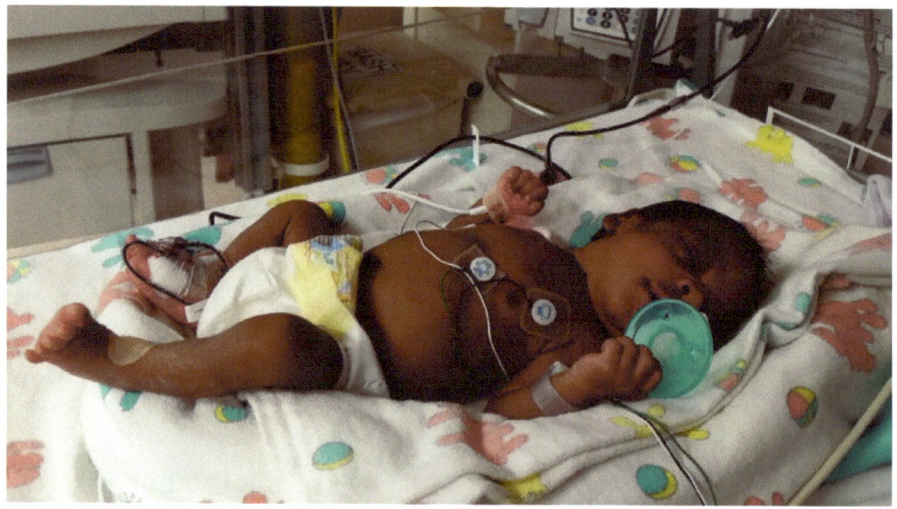

The next few days after the transfusion, Asa's white blood cell count had increased. The doctor would continue to monitor his blood count for another week, and if all were well, he would soon be able to come home. Prior to Asa's discharge, the doctor set up a series of follow-up appointments and routine checkups.

# Asa's Home

On May 26, 2014, after spending six weeks in the hospital, Asa was finally able to come home. My family was so excited. This time around, it was different. We now had a newborn baby and a seven-year-old son. My husband and I took the first few weeks to become acclimated to the feedings every three hours. We developed a schedule that worked for us. We also wanted to make sure Justin still had a sense of normalcy. Justin was now a big brother, but I did not want him to feel left out or that he was no longer important. So, we made sure that Justin had his time with us and was able to do some of the things he wanted to do. Justin wanted to help take care of his little brother, and he was very helpful in assisting me with Asa.

Similar to Justin, at each appointment, the doctor charted Asa's weight, length, and head circumference and would compare the numbers on the chronological and adjusted charts to determine if he were growing correctly. As part of the hospital's protocol for premature babies, Asa was also referred to the Alta Regional Program for early intervention to enhance the growth and development in children. Asa had a series of appointments with his primary care physician, occupational and physical therapists, and specialty doctors in the High-Risk Infant Follow-Up Clinic. Every six months, the doctors tested Asa's growth and development.

I went back to work when Asa was four months old. This time, instead of putting him in an in-home daycare, my mother-in-law said she wanted to watch him for us. Even though I was not ready to go back to work, I knew Asa would be in good hands.

When Asa was about one and a half years old, he began to learn how to walk. He also started out walking on his toes. I really believe that walking on your toes is a hereditary trait in my family, so I was not surprised when I saw Asa walking in this manner.

After several appointments with the physical therapist, she determined that, since Asa had good range of motion in his calves and ankles, no more appointments were necessary. She gave us a series of exercises to do with Asa to help keep his calves from becoming stiff. Not only does Asa walk on his toes, he also runs on his toes as well.

After the two-year mark, Asa was considered to be on right on track according to all the charts and graphs. The only concern the doctor had was that Asa was not saying as many words as she thought he should. Although she signed off on the completion of the appointments at the two-year mark, she recommended that I take a class to help Asa better communicate. Over the next few months, Asa's vocabulary began to increase. The class provided helpful tips and gave me an opportunity to talk with other parents whose children were at various stages of communication.

My mother-in-law has been very instrumental in Asa's learning advancement. She ordered a Hooked-on Phonics set that included DVDs, flash cards, stickers, and workbooks to help Asa learn his alphabet, letters, colors, and numbers. She played the DVDs and read to Asa every day. Two of Asa's favorite books to read were *Pop, Pop, Pop* and the *Letter Hunt*. When Asa was two years old, he learned how to use YouTube and started to pull up Elmo videos.

# Life Today

Today, Justin is ten years old and just started the fifth grade. He is very intelligent, inquisitive, and mild mannered. He has done well academically each school year as well as socially. He has a good sense of humor. Justin has an advanced brown belt in martial arts and developed a love for other sports such as basketball and soccer. He loves action movies and fast cars, and he enjoys playing video games with his cousins and friends. I can see a lot of myself in him. He always wants to do well and is very hard on himself when he messes up or does not get the grade he wants.

As he gets older, I've noticed he is becoming more mature. Justin is a very protective of Asa and tries to keep him out of trouble. Asa is three years old and just started preschool. He is very inquisitive and active. He loves to run and jump. He recognizes his letters, numbers, and shapes and also knows the letters in sign language. He is tech savvy. He knows how to play games, take selfies, and navigate through YouTube on the smartphones and the iPad. He is very independent and wants to do everything on his own. I am often told that Asa is a replica of my husband when he was a little boy. They are both church babies and active participants in Kidz Kingdom and Children's Church.

I was really concerned that the seven-year age difference between Justin and Asa would be a problem, but I was wrong. They are inseparable. They are very close and love being around each other. Asa follows Justin around the house, takes his toys, and wants to go everywhere Justin goes. I enjoy watching them grow up together. I am also grateful that a large number of family and friends who loves and supports them now surrounds them.

God allowed my family to survive these experiences, and my husband and I are working hard to provide our sons with the resources they will need to be successful in life. No matter what you go through, know that God is always with you and will never put more on you than you can bear. If God can do it for my family, he can do it for yours as well.

# Kyna Kemp

# Resources for Parents of Premature Babies

Below is a list of hospitals and organizations that specialize in assisting families of premature children.

<u>Hospitals</u>
Kaiser Roseville
https://thrive.kaiserpermanente.org

Mercy Health System
https://mercyhealthsystem.org

Mercy Hospital/Dignity Health
www.dignityhealth.org

Sutter Medical Center
www.suttermedicalcenter.org

UC Davis Medical Center
www.ucdmc.usdavis.edu

<u>Services</u>
Alta California Regional Center
www.altaregional.org

Brave Beginnings
www.bravebeginnings.org

Coalition for Infant Health
www.infanthealth.org

Graham's Foundation: Fighting for Premature Babies
www.grahamsfoundation.org

Hand to Hold
www.handtohold.org

March of Dimes
www.marchofdimes.org

Miracle Babies
www.miraclebabies.org

Nationwide Children's Hospital
www.nationwidechildrens.org

Preemie Parent Alliance
www.preemieparentalliance.org

# **Notes**

Use this section to write down your concerns, questions and reflections.

www.ingramcontent.com/pod-product-compliance
Lightning Source LLC
Chambersburg PA
CBHW041526090426
42736CB00035B/29